Very little is needed to make a happy life. It is all within yourself, in your way of thinking.

Marcus Aurelius

A weed is a plant whose virtues have not been discovered.

Ralph Waldo Emerson

To be able to look back upon
one's past life with satisfaction
is to live twice.

Martial

He enjoys true leisure who has
time to improve his soul's
estate.

Henry David Thoreau

We are shaped and fashioned
by what we love.
  Johann Wolfgang von Goethe

The greater man, the greater
courtesy.
  Alfred, Lord Tennyson

There is much satisfaction in
work well done; praise is
sweet; but there can be no
happiness equal to the joy of
finding a heart that understands.
Victor Robinson

The plainest sign of wisdom is
a continual cheerfulness: her
state is like that of things in
the regions above the moon,
always clear and serene.
Michel de Montaigne

It is better for you to be free
of fear lying upon a pallet,
than to have a golden couch
and a rich table and be full of
trouble.

Epicurus

Faith, like light, should always
be simple and unbending;
while love, like warmth, should
beam forth on every side, and
bend to every necessity of our
brethren.

Martin Luther

My words fly up, my thoughts
    remain below:
Words without thoughts never
    to heaven go.

> *William Shakespeare,*
> Hamlet

Nothing in life is more
wonderful than faith—the one
great moving force which we
can neither weigh in the
balance nor test in the crucible.

> *Sir William Osler*

Human felicity is produced
not so much by great pieces of
good fortune that seldom
happen as by little advantages
that occur every day.

Benjamin Franklin

Always remember to forget
The troubles that passed away,
But never forget to remember
The blessings that come each
day.

Anonymous

Life is short and we have not too much time for gladdening the hearts of those who are traveling the dark way with us. Oh, be swift to love! Make haste to be kind.

Henri Frederic Amiel

Quick sensitiveness is inseparable from a ready understanding.

Joseph Addison

Surely there is something in the unruffled calm of nature that overawes our little anxieties and doubts; the sight of the deep-blue sky and the clustering stars above seems to impart a quiet to the mind.

Tryon Edwards

Good thoughts, even if they are forgotten, do not perish.

Publilius Syrus

Go confidently in the direction
of your dreams! Live the life
you've imagined! As you
simplify your life, the laws of
the universe will be simpler;
solitude will not be solitude,
poverty will not be poverty,
nor weakness weakness.

Henry David Thoreau

I avoid looking forward or
backward, and try to keep
looking *upward*.

Charlotte Brontë

It is not written, blessed is he that *feedeth* the poor, but he that *considereth* the poor. A little thought and a little kindness are often worth more than a great deal of money.

John Ruskin

Happiness grows at our own firesides, and is not to be picked in strangers' gardens.

Douglas Jerrold

Have courage for the great sorrows of life and patience for the small ones. And when you have finished your daily task, go to sleep in peace. God is awake.

Victor Hugo

Happy is the man who has broken the chains which hurt the mind, and has given up worrying once and for all.

Ovid

Next to love, sympathy is the divinest passion of the human heart.

Edmund Burke

The love of learning, the
sequestered nooks,
And all the sweet serenity
of books.
Henry Wadsworth Longfellow

A teacher who can arouse a feeling for one single good action, for one single good poem, accomplishes more than he who fills our memory with rows on rows of natural objects, classified with name and form.

Johann Wolfgang von Goethe

They are never alone that are accompanied with noble thoughts.

Sir Philip Sidney

There are two worlds; the world that we can measure with line and rule, and the world that we feel with our hearts and imagination.

Leigh Hunt

A merry heart doeth good like a medicine: but a broken spirit drieth the bones.

Proverbs 17:22

First keep thyself in peace and then shalt thou be able to pacify others. A peaceable man doth more good than he that is well learned.

Thomas à Kempis

A boy's will is the wind's will, And the thoughts of youth are long, long thoughts.

Henry Wadsworth Longfellow

Enjoy the blessings of this day, if God sends them; and the evils of it bear patiently and sweetly; for this day only is ours; we are dead to yesterday, and we are not yet born to the morrow.

Jeremy Taylor

The grand essentials to happiness in this life are something to do, something to love, and something to hope for.

Joseph Addison

Grief is a matter of relativity;
the sorrow should be estimated
by its proportion to the
sorrower; a gash is as painful
to one as an amputation to
another.

Francis Thompson

All the darkness of the world
cannot put out the light of one
small candle.

Anonymous

Tranquil pleasures last the longest.

Christian Bovée

If I can stop one heart from
    breaking,
I shall not live in vain:
If I can ease one life the aching,
Or cool one pain,
Or help one fainting robin
Unto his nest again,
I shall not live in vain.

Emily Dickinson

Give me, kind Heaven,
   a private station,
A mind serene for
   contemplation:
Title and profit I resign;
The post of honour shall
   be mine.

              John Gay

Nothing happens to any man
which he is not formed by
nature to bear.

        Marcus Aurelius

The glow of one warm thought
is to me worth more than
money.

Thomas Jefferson

In this world second thoughts,
it seems, are best.

Euripides

Some of your hurts you have
   cured,
      And the sharpest you still
      have survived,
But what torments of grief you
   endured
      From evils which never
      arrived!

Ralph Waldo Emerson

It is far easier to be wise for
others than to be so for
oneself.

Duc de La Rochefoucauld

All higher motives, ideals, conceptions, sentiments in a man are of no account if they do not come forward to strengthen him for the better discharge of the duties which devolve upon him in the ordinary affairs of life.

Henry Ward Beecher

The most wasted of days is that in which one has not laughed.

Sebastian R. N. Chamfort

The most disastrous times
have produced the greatest
minds. The purest metal comes
of the most ardent furnace,
the most brilliant lightning
comes of the darkest clouds.

*François René
de Chateaubriand*

Habit is a cable; we weave a
thread of it every day, and at
last we can not break it.

Horace Mann

Ideals are like stars; you will not succeed in touching them with your hands. But like the seafaring man on the desert of waters, you choose them as your guides, and following them you will reach your destiny.

Carl Schurz

There's enough opportunity to live life on the edge without being self-destructive.

Patrick Swayze

Who is narrow of vision
cannot be big-hearted; who is
narrow of spirit cannot take
long, easy strides.

Chinese Proverb

No soul is desolate as long as
there is a human being for
whom it can feel trust and
reverence.

George Eliot

Make a rule, and pray God to help you to keep it, never, if possible, to lie down at night without being able to say, "I have made one human being, at least, a little wiser, a little happier, or a little better this day."

Charles Kingsley

As if we could kill time without injuring eternity!

Henry David Thoreau

The greatest comfort of my old
age, and that which gives me
the highest satisfaction, is the
pleasing remembrance of the
many benefits and friendly
offices I have done to others.

Cato

Happiness never lays its finger
on its pulse. If we attempt to
steal a glimpse of its features
it disappears.

Alexander Smith

Oh, what a little thing can turn
A heavy heart from sighs to
   song!
A smile can make the world
   less stern,
A word can cause the soul
   to burn
With glow of heaven, all
   night long.

Anonymous

He who doesn't accept the
conditions of life sells his
soul.

Charles Baudelaire

Lift up one hand to heaven
and thank your stars if they
have given you the proper
sense to enable you to
appreciate the inconceivably
droll situations in which we
catch our fellow creatures.

Sir William Osler

Who reflects too much will
accomplish little.

Friedrich von Schiller

Work spares us from three great evils: boredom, vice and need.

Voltaire

A mental waste-paper basket! Everyone should keep one and the older he grows the more things will he the more promptly consign to it—torn up to irrecoverable tatters.

Samuel Butler

A grain of sand leads to the fall of a mountain when the moment has come for the mountain to fall.

Ernest Renan

All intelligent thoughts have already been thought; what is necessary is only to try to think them again.

Johann Wolfgang von Goethe

Those who have the largest
hearts have the soundest
understandings; and he is the
truest philosopher who can
forget himself.

William Hazlitt

Blessed are the happiness
makers; blessed are they that
remove friction, that make the
courses of life smooth and the
converse of men gentle.

Henry Ward Beecher

How awful to reflect that what people say of us is true!

Logan Pearsall Smith

There was never a person who did anything worth doing that did not receive more than he gave.

Henry Ward Beecher

I leave this notice on my door
For each accustomed visitor:
"I am gone into the fields
To take what this sweet hour
    yields;
Reflection, you may come
    tomorrow,
Sit by the fireside of Sorrow.
You with the unpaid bill,
    Despair,
You tiresome verse-reciter,
    Care,
I will pay you in the grave,
Death will listen, to your stave.
Expectation, too, be off!
Today is for itself enough."

Percy Bysshe Shelley

He that thinks himself the
happiest man really is so.

C. C. Colton

Mirth is like a flash of
lightning that breaks through
a gloom of clouds, and glitters
for a moment; cheerfulness
keeps up a kind of daylight in
the mind, and fills it with a
steady and perpetual serenity.

Joseph Addison

Prayer does not change God,
but changes him who prays.

Sören Kierkegaard

If we could read the secret
history of our enemies, we
should find in each man's life
sorrow and suffering enough
to disarm all hostility.

Henry Wadsworth Longfellow

The improvement of our way
of life is more important than
the spreading of it.

Charles A. Lindbergh

The weakest among us has a
gift, however seemingly trivial,
which is peculiar to him, and
which worthily used, will be a
gift to his race forever.

John Ruskin

Two chambers has the heart,
Wherein dwell Joy and Sorrow;
When Joy awakes in one,
Then slumbers Sorrow in
   the other.
O Joy, take care!
Speak softly,
Lest you awaken Sorrow.

Herman Neuman

Weeping may endure for a
night, but joy cometh in the
morning.

Psalms 30:5

Things past belong to memory
alone; Things future are the
property of hope.

John Home

A wonderful fact to reflect
upon, that every human
creature is constituted to be
that profound secret and
mystery to every other.

Charles Dickens

The man who makes no
mistakes does not usually
make anything.
            Bishop W. C. Magee

The pleasantest things in the
world are pleasant thoughts;
and the great art of life is to
have as many of them as
possible.
            Michel de Montaigne

Endeavor to be patient in bearing the defects and infirmities of others, of what sort soever they be; for thou thyself also hast many failings which must be borne with by others.

Thomas à Kempis

It is tranquil people who accomplish much.

Henry David Thoreau

The ideal man bears the
accidents of life with dignity
and grace, making the best of
circumstances.

Aristotle

Each heart is a world.—You
find all within yourself that
you find without.—To know
yourself you have only to set
down a true statement of those
that ever loved or hated you.

Johann Kasper Lavater

The supreme happiness of life is the conviction that we are loved, loved for ourselves, or rather loved in spite of ourselves.

Victor Hugo

The real problem is not whether machines think but whether men do.

B. F. Skinner

To know things as they are is
better than to believe things
as they seem.

Tom Wicker

Leave something to wish for,
so as not to be miserable from
very happiness.

Baltasar Gracián

The natural flights of the
human mind are not from
pleasure to pleasure, but from
hope to hope.

Samuel Johnson

Coming together is a beginning;
keeping together is progress;
working together is success.

Henry Ford

The perception of the Comic is a tie of sympathy with other men, a pledge of sanity. We must learn by laughter as well as by tears and terror.

Ralph Waldo Emerson

I confess freely to you, I could never look long upon a monkey, without very mortifying reflections.

William Congreve

God grant that not only the love of liberty but a thorough knowledge of the rights of man may pervade all the nations of the earth, so that a philosopher may set his foot anywhere on its surface and say: "This is my country."

Benjamin Franklin

I love tranquil solitude
  And such society
As is quiet, wise and good.

Percy Bysshe Shelley

The best part of human
language, properly so called, is
derived from reflection on the
acts of the mind itself.

Samuel Taylor Coleridge

It is with life as with a play—it
matters not how long the
action is spun out, but how
good the acting is.

Seneca

The best thing to give to your enemy is forgiveness; to an opponent, tolerance; to a friend, your heart; to your child, a good example; to a father, deference; to your mother, conduct that will make her proud of you; to yourself, respect; to all men, charity.

John Balfour

We shall see but a little way if we require to understand what we see.

Henry David Thoreau

To doubt everything or to
believe everything are two
equally convenient solutions;
both dispense with the
necessity of reflection.

Jules Henri Poincaré

Correction does much, but
encouragement does more.
Encouragement after censure
is as the sun after a shower.

Johann Wolfgang von Goethe

A contented mind is the greatest blessing a man can enjoy in this world; and if, in the present life, his happiness arises from the subduing of his desires, it will rise to the next from the gratification of them.

Joseph Addison

The human race has one really effective weapon, and that is laughter.

Mark Twain

It seems to me we can never
give up longing and wishing
while we are thoroughly alive.
There are certain things we
feel to be beautiful and good,
and we must hunger after
them.

George Eliot

He is a wise man who does not
grieve for the things which he
has not, but rejoices for those
which he has.

Epictetus

Every man, however obscure,
however far removed from the
general recognition, is one of
a group of men impressible for
good, and impressible for evil,
and it is in the nature of
things that he can not really
improve himself without in
some degree improving other
men.

Charles Dickens

A moment's insight is some-
times worth a life's experience.
Oliver Wendell Holmes

The talent of success is
nothing more than doing what
you can do well, and doing
well whatever you do.
  Henry Wadsworth Longfellow

Some people are always
grumbling because roses have
thorns. I am thankful that
thorns have roses.
                Alphonse Karr

A man can know nothing of
mankind without knowing
something of himself. Self-
knowledge is the property of
that man whose passions have
their full play, but who
ponders over their results

Benjamin Disraeli

A great man is he who has not
lost the heart of a child.

Mencius

Music, when soft voices die,
Vibrates in the memory;
Odors, when sweet violets
   sicken,
Live within the sense they
   quicken.

Rose leaves, when the rose
   is dead,
Are heaped for the beloved's
   bed;
And so thy thoughts, when
   thou art gone,
Love itself shall slumber on.

Percy Bysshe Shelley

And when we come to think of it, goodness *is* uneventful. It does not flash, it glows. It is deep, quiet, and very simple. It passes not with oratory, it is commonly foreign to riches, nor does it often sit in the places of the mighty: but may be felt in the touch of a friendly hand or the look of a kindly eye.

David Grayson

Most people don't plan to fail—they fail to plan.

Anonymous

Sacred cows make the tastiest hamburger.

Abbie Hoffman

We need to see the homeless for who they are and see that we need them as much as they need us. Only by recognizing that we're all roommates in the house of life together can we clean up our house and make it livable again.

William Lawyer

Troubles are often the tools by which God fashions us for better things.

Henry Ward Beecher

Life is too short to waste
In critic peep or cynic bark,
Quarrel or reprimand:
'Twill soon be dark;
Up! mind thine own aim, and
God speed the mark!

Ralph Waldo Emerson

In order that people may be
happy in their work, these
three things are needed: They
must be fit for it: They must
not do too much of it: And
they must have a sense of
success in it.

John Ruskin

Imparting knowledge is only
lighting other men's candles at
our lamp without depriving
ourselves of any flame.

Jane Porter

If you don't learn from your mistakes, there's no sense making them.

Anonymous

Sunlight—floating through the whiteness warms the icy river of my dreams.

Japanese haiku

It is surely better to pardon too much than to condemn too much.

George Eliot

I am a great believer in luck. The harder I work, the more of it I seem to have.

Coleman Cox

No one is useless in this world
who lightens the burden of it
to anyone else.

Charles Dickens

Tact is a gift; it is likewise a
grace. As a gift it may or may
not have fallen to our share; as
a grace we are bound either to
possess or to acquire it.

Christina G. Rossetti

Wide rough river playing tag
with the wind. Never
catching its wild friend.
Japanese haiku

For of all sad words of tongue
or pen,
The saddest are these:
"It might have been!"
John Greenleaf Whittier

Happiness is as a butterfly,
which, when pursued, is always
beyond our grasp, but which,
if you will sit down quietly,
may alight upon you.
            Nathaniel Hawthorne

The story of any one man's
real experience finds its
startling parallel in that of
every one of us.
            James Russell Lowell

Certain thoughts are prayers.
There are moments when,
whatever be the attitude of the
body, the soul is on its knees.

Victor Hugo

Sometimes it proves the highest
understanding not to
understand.

Baltasar Gracián

What do we live for, if it is not
to make life less difficult to
others?

George Eliot

Give what you have. To some
one, it may be better than you
dare to think.

Henry Wadsworth Longfellow

There is a certain relief in
change, even though it be from
bad to worse; as I have found
in traveling in a stage coach,
that it is often a comfort to
shift one's position and be
bruised in a new place.

Washington Irving

It is not how much we have,
but how much we enjoy, that
makes happiness.

Charles Haddon Spurgeon

He that would live in peace
    and ease
Must not speak all he knows
    nor judge all he sees.
                Benjamin Franklin

Gladness can scarcely be a
solitary thing. The very life of
praise seems choral; it is more
than one bounded heart can
utter.

                Dora Greenwell

He that is well in peace is not suspicious of any.

Thomas à Kempis

An inexhaustible good nature is one of the most precious gifts of heaven, spreading itself like oil over the troubled sea of thought, and keeping the mind smooth and equable in the roughest weather.

Washington Irving

God grant me the Serenity to accept the things I cannot change, Courage to change the things I can, and Wisdom to know the difference.

Reinhold Niebuhr

Let thy discontents be secret.

Benjamin Franklin

Advice is like snow; the softer
it falls, the longer it dwells
upon, and the deeper it sinks
into the mind.

Samuel Taylor Coleridge

The world is a looking-glass,
and gives back to every man
the reflection of his own face.
Frown at it, and it in turn will
look sourly upon you; laugh at
it and with it, and it is a jolly,
kind companion.

William Makepeace Thackeray

I'll not willingly offend,
  Nor be easily offended;
What's amiss I'll strive to mend,
  And endure what can't be
  mended.

Isaac Watts

My crown is in my heart,
  not on my head;
Not deck'd with diamonds
  and Indian stones,
Nor to be seen: my crown
  is called content;
A crown it is that seldom
  kings enjoy.

William Shakespeare

There is no greater mistake in the world than the looking upon every sort of nonsense as want of sense.

Leigh Hunt

Smooth runs the water where the brook is deep.

William Shakespeare

Before we passionately wish
for anything, we should care-
fully examine the happiness of
its possessor.

      Duc de La Rochefoucauld

Life is a dead-end street.

      H. L. Mencken